Uranus

WITHDRAWN

E L A I N E   L A N D A U

Children's Press®
A Division of Scholastic Inc.
New York   Toronto   London   Auckland   Sydney
Mexico City   New Delhi   Hong Kong

Content Consultant

Michelle Yehling

Astronomy Education Consultant

Aurora, Illinois

Reading Consultant

Linda Cornwell

Literacy Consultant

Carmel, Indiana

Library of Congress Cataloging-in-Publication Data

Landau, Elaine.
Uranus / by Elaine Landau.
    p. cm.—(A true book)
Includes bibliographical references and index.
ISBN-13: 978-0-531-12569-4 (lib. bdg.)   978-0-531-14797-9 (pbk.)
ISBN-10: 0-531-12569-6 (lib. bdg.)   0-531-14797-5 (pbk.)
1. Uranus (Planet)—Juvenile literature. I. Title. II. Series.
QB681.L36 2008
523.47—dc22   2007012258

All rights reserved. Published in 2008 by Children's Press, an imprint of Scholastic Inc.
Published simultaneously in Canada. Printed in the United States of America.
SCHOLASTIC, CHILDREN'S PRESS, A TRUE BOOK, and associated logos are trademarks and/or registered trademarks of Scholastic Inc.
1 2 3 4 5 6 7 8 9 10 R 17 16 15 14 13 12 11 10 09

Find the Truth!

Everything you are about to read is true *except* for one of the sentences on this page.

Which one is **TRUE**?

T or F   There are no rings around Uranus.

T or F   Uranus is the first planet that was discovered by using a telescope.

 Find the answer in this book.

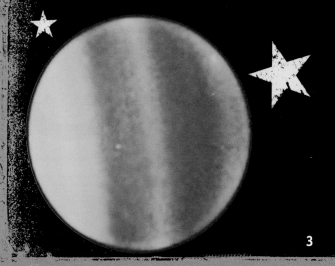

Contents

THE **BIG** TRUTH!

Greetings, Space Creatures

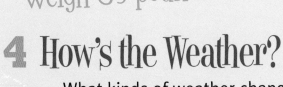

A person who weighs 100 pounds on Earth would weigh 89 pounds on Uranus.

This artwork shows *Voyager 2* approaching Uranus in 1996.

You might be able to spot Uranus on a clear, dark night if you know exactly where to look. To get a view like this one, you would need a telescope.

Uranus

CHAPTER 1

A Trip to Uranus

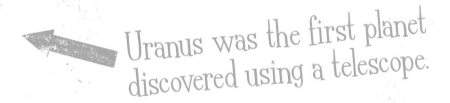

Uranus was the first planet discovered using a telescope.

Uranus is a mysterious planet. The first six planets in our **solar system** can be seen easily without telescopes. So they were discovered in ancient times. People did not know about Uranus before telescopes were invented. Even when **astronomers** had telescopes, many thought Uranus was just another star in the sky.

If you were going to travel from Earth to Uranus, how would you get there? Blast off and head away from the sun. Keep going for at least 1.7 billion miles (2.7 billion kilometers)!

Uranus is the second-to-last planet from the sun. Because it is so far away, Uranus doesn't receive very much energy from the sun. That makes it a cold, cold planet.

All spacecraft need powerful rockets to get off the ground.

There is a joke about this greenish-blue planet. People say that the planet got so cold it turned blue. That joke is not really true. The color actually comes from the gases that surround the planet. But

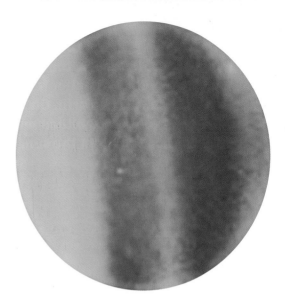

A gas called methane gives Uranus its blue color. Methane looks blue when sunlight hits it.

the planet is cold enough to turn *you* blue. The temperature of the **atmosphere** around Uranus is hundreds of degrees below zero! An atmosphere is the blanket of gases that surrounds a planet or moon.

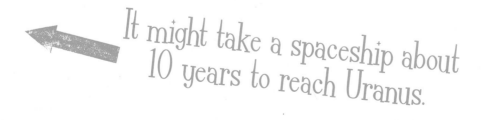

It might take a spaceship about 10 years to reach Uranus.

This drawing shows the sun lighting up Uranus. In reality, the sun would look many times smaller from Uranus than it looks from Earth. On average, Uranus is about 1.8 billion miles (2.9 billion km) from the sun.

CHAPTER 2

Uranus in the Solar System

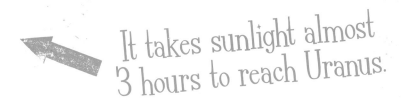

It takes sunlight almost 3 hours to reach Uranus.

The solar system contains the sun and eight planets. The planets are Mercury, Venus, Earth, Mars, Jupiter, Saturn, Uranus, and Neptune. Mercury is the planet closest to the sun, while Neptune is farthest away. Our solar system contains other objects, too, such as moons, **comets**, **asteroids**, and at least three **dwarf planets**.

Uranus's Solar System

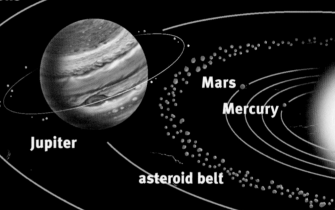
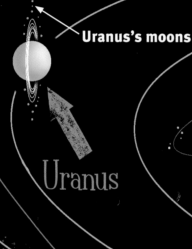

Pluto (dwarf planet)

Uranus's moons

Uranus

Jupiter

Mars

Mercury

asteroid belt

Uranus

- Seventh planet from the sun
- Third-largest planet
- Diameter: 31,764 mi. (51,118 km)
- Length of a day: About 17 Earth hours
- Length of a year: About 84 Earth years

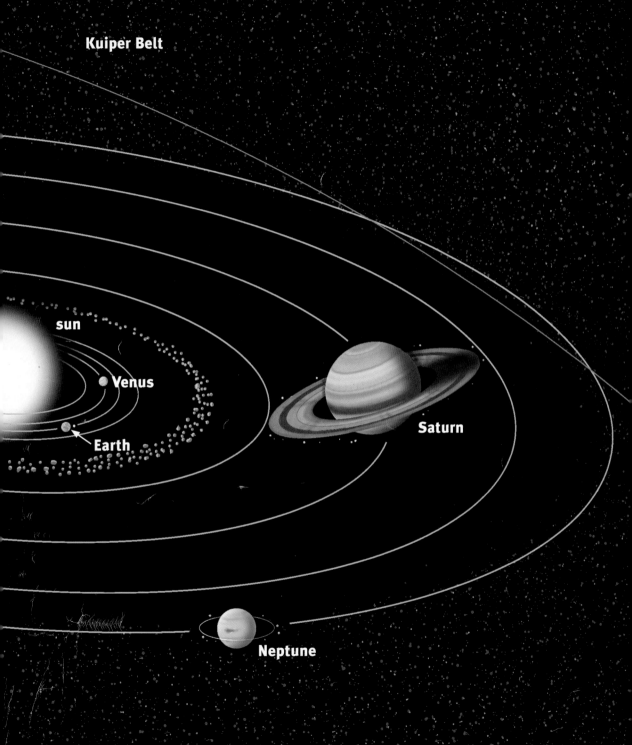

Kuiper Belt

sun

Venus

Earth

Saturn

Neptune

If you are 10 years old on Earth, you would be less than one year old on Uranus!

Uranus has a longer year than Earth, but it has a shorter day.

What's One Year?

Like all the planets in our solar system, Uranus **orbits**, or travels around, the sun. Each planet makes this orbit in a flattened circle called an ellipse (ee-LIPS).

The time it takes a planet to circle the sun once equals one year on that planet. Earth takes about 365 days to complete its orbit around the sun. However, Uranus takes much longer because it's farther from the sun than Earth is. Uranus needs about 84 Earth years to travel around the sun just once.

Turning Sideways

The planets in our solar system orbit the sun. They also **rotate**, or spin, on an **axis**. An axis is an imaginary line through the center of a planet.

The time it takes a planet to rotate once equals one day on that planet. Earth's rotation takes about 24 hours. Uranus takes only about 17 Earth hours to rotate once. So one day on Uranus is about 17 Earth hours long.

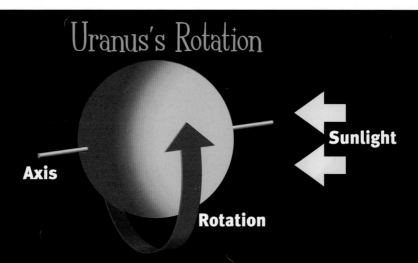

Uranus's Rotation

Axis

Sunlight

Rotation

The red arrow above shows the direction of Uranus's rotation. Uranus is tilted onto its side so its axis runs side to side, not up-and-down as it does in most planets. The sun lights up half of the planet at any time.

This photo of Uranus was taken by cameras
on a spacecraft called *Voyager 2*.

Most planets rotate like spinning tops. The axis runs up and down. Uranus is different. It is like a top that fell onto its side and kept spinning.

Why is Uranus tilted? No one knows for sure. Some astronomers think that Uranus was hit by a planet-sized object billions of years ago. That could have knocked the planet on its side.

This tilt does strange things to day and night on the planet. One pole, or end, of the planet is in daylight for 42 Earth years at a time. That's the time it takes Uranus to move halfway through its orbit. Then that pole gets 42 years of darkness. Farther from the poles, it gets light and dark every day.

Near Uranus's poles, the sun takes 42 years to rise or set!

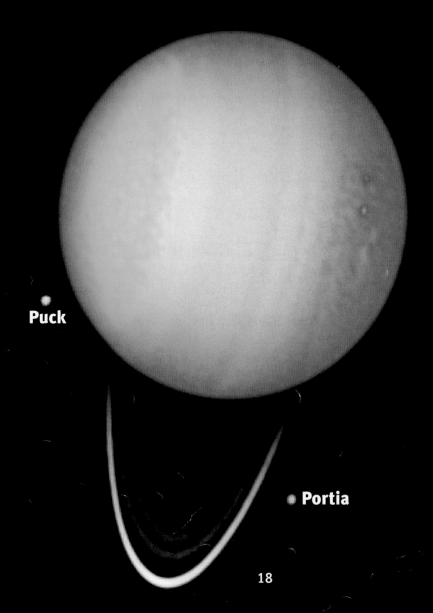

The Hubble Space Telescope took this picture of Uranus, its rings, and three of its moons in August 2003.

Puck

Portia

Ariel

18

CHAPTER 3

What's It Like on Uranus?

Uranus's rings are made partly of smashed moons.

It's hard to learn about a planet that is billions of miles away. Even through a large backyard telescope, Uranus looks like a greenish-blue disk. But scientists have cameras on huge telescopes that can get a better view. They also have information from a spacecraft that has gotten closer to Uranus. What have the scientists learned?

Uranus doesn't have a rocky surface like Earth.
The giant, cloudy planet is called a gas giant.
Jupiter, Saturn, and Neptune are also gas giants.
They are made mostly of liquid and gas.

About 63 Earths could fit inside Uranus.

Neptune

Uranus

Saturn

Jupiter

This image shows the relative sizes of the gas giants. Jupiter is the largest gas giant as well as the largest planet.

Who Discovered Uranus?

William Herschel was a conductor and music teacher in England. In his spare time, he built hundreds of telescopes and studied the stars.

In 1781, Herschel spotted a new object with his telescope. He knew that planets move across the sky and stars don't. By tracking the movements of this object, he and other scientists realized it was a previously undiscovered planet.

After discovering Uranus, William Herschel was appointed the King's Astronomer to King George III in 1782.

Herschel named the new object Georgium Sidus (JOR-jee-um SY-dus), or "George's star," after King George III of Great Britain. Later, it was named after a god, like the other planets. Uranus is the Greek god of the heavens.

The Pressure Is On

The atmosphere of Uranus is a mixture of gases. Inside the planet is a mixture of gases, liquid, ice, and rock. "Ice" does not always mean frozen water. Uranus's ice is made of the same gases that are found in the rest of the planet.

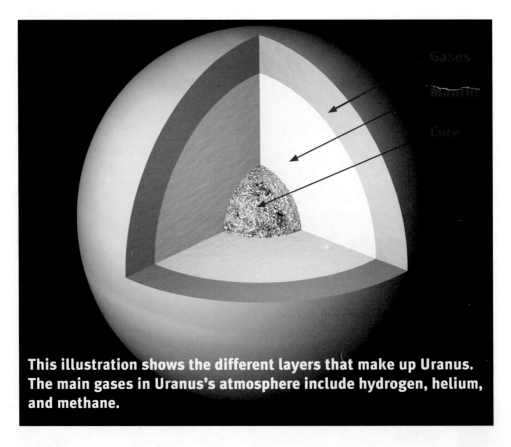

Gases

Mantle

Core

This illustration shows the different layers that make up Uranus. The main gases in Uranus's atmosphere include hydrogen, helium, and methane.

Ice in Uranus is formed from the pressure of the gases above it. Gases in the atmosphere press down on the gases below them. This pressure squeezes the gases until they turn into a thick, icy liquid. Most of the planet is made up of this cold mush. It forms a layer called the mantle.

The pressure is highest in the center of the planet. Astronomers believe that pressure squeezes the liquid into a solid. Uranus's core is probably made of rock and metal. Pressure can also heat things up. The core of the cold planet is blazing hot.

The inner part of Uranus can reach 12,600°F!

Greetings, Space Creatures

What would you say to an alien? Scientists have recorded a solid gold disk full of greetings for aliens. A spacecraft called *Voyager 2* is carrying this disk into deep space. On the disk is a sampling of sounds and sights from Earth.

Scientists don't expect the spacecraft to meet any aliens. But they included instructions for playing the disk, just in case.

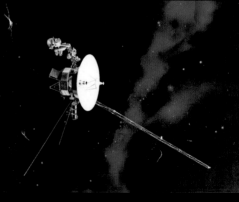

It will take Voyager 2 40,000 years to reach the nearest star outside our solar system.

The Voyager golden record has been traveling through space since 1977.

What would you hear if you played it?

- "Hello" in 55 languages
- 115 nature sounds, including ocean waves, wind, birdcalls, and whale sounds
- Songs from 27 countries
- A message from then-president Jimmy Carter of the United States: "This is a present from a small, distant world, a token of our sounds, our science, our images, our music, our thoughts, and our feelings. We are attempting to survive our time so we may live into yours."

Uranus's tilt makes the rings run up
and down, rather than side to side.
The bright white and blue spots
in this image are clouds above the
planet.

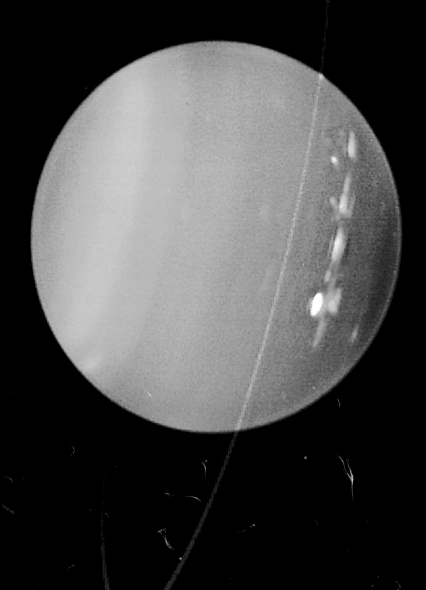

CHAPTER 4

How's the Weather?

The average temperature in Uranus's clouds is more than 200 degrees colder than the coldest temperature on Earth!

Think about how much the sun warms Earth. Even on a chilly day, you may be able to feel the sun's warmth. And even on the coldest day, the sun keeps Earth warm enough for life to exist. Now imagine Uranus deep in space, 19 times as far from the sun as Earth is. Uranus is one cold planet!

Earth and Uranus both have clouds in their atmospheres. The clouds we see in Earth's sky are made of water droplets. Clouds on Uranus are made of gases and ice. These clouds cover the planet every day.

The winds on Uranus are so strong that they blow the upper clouds at great speeds. The winds blow the clouds into long shapes. They form a striped pattern all around the planet.

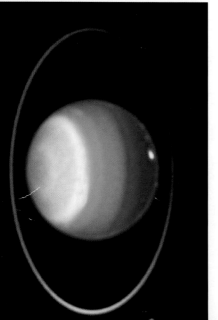

It's extremely cold at Uranus's cloud tops. The temperature there is about −357°F (−216°C). However, toward the planet's center, the temperature rises.

Winds blowing Uranus's upper clouds can reach speeds of almost 370 miles (600 km) per hour. This photo was taken with special cameras that show the clouds in false color.

The Hubble Space Telescope stands eight stories high and weighs 300 tons.

The Hubble Space Telescope has been orbiting Earth since 1990.

For many years, the weather on Uranus seemed to remain constant. Some astronomers even said that the weather there was boring to study. But not anymore! In the late 1990s, the powerful Hubble Space Telescope, followed by other telescopes, began to spot many weather changes on Uranus. Now it seems as though new clouds are forming on the planet. The clouds are moving faster than ever. They are also rapidly changing shape. Astronomers have even found new storms on the planet. Astronomers are keeping a close eye on all these changes.

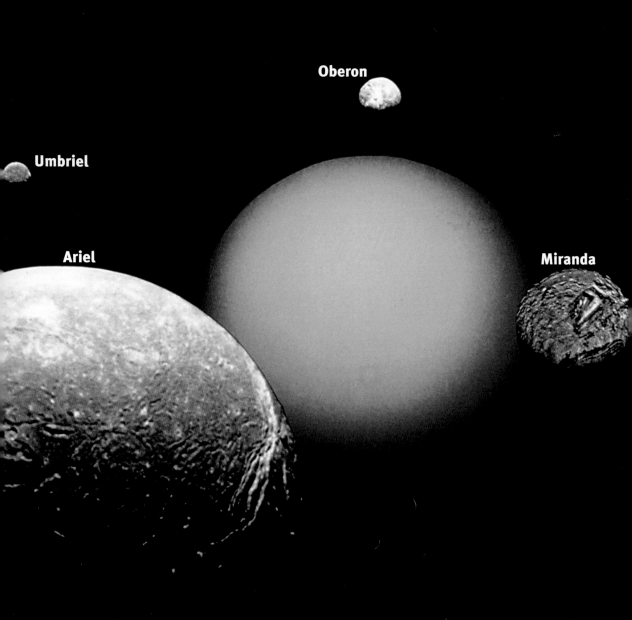

Oberon

Umbriel

Ariel

Miranda

CHAPTER 5

Moons and Rings

Many of Uranus's moons have been named after characters from the works of playwright William Shakespeare.

Earth has one moon. Imagine if you could look up and see many moons! Or imagine what Earth would look like if it had rings around it. Astronomers have discovered 27 moons orbiting Uranus. There are 13 rings, as well.

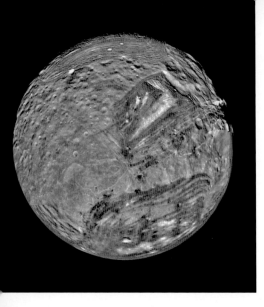

Miranda was discovered in 1948. Astronomers aren't sure what created its valleys and cliffs.

Most of Uranus's moons are small. Five of them are larger, icy bodies. Let's take a look at Uranus's five major moons.

Miranda (muh-RAN-duh) is the major moon closest to Uranus. It's made of ice and rock. Miranda has deep canyons. One is more than 12 times deeper than Earth's Grand Canyon. Miranda's surface is covered with valleys, cliffs, and strange-looking grooves. Some astronomers describe its surface as looking like the swirls and grooves in the frosting of a cake.

None of Uranus's moons has an atmosphere.

Ariel (A-ree-uhl) is Uranus's brightest moon. Its surface has a few large craters, or holes, along with many small ones. This moon also has many long valleys. Astronomers think the moon had a very hot interior a long time ago. But the moon is freezing cold now. The valleys may have formed while the moon was cooling down, like cracks in an ice cube.

Umbriel (UHM-bree-uhl) is the darkest of Uranus's five major moons. Near the moon's top is a bright ring. Astronomers call it the **"fluorescent Cheerio."** Astronomers are not sure what the ring is.

This illustration, shows the relative sizes of Uranus (far left) and its five largest moons.

Moons and Rings?

Which planet in the solar system has the most moons? Which planet has the most rings? Check this chart and see.

Planet	Number of Moons	Number of Rings
Mercury	0	0
Venus	0	0
Earth	1	0
Mars	2	0
Jupiter	63	4
Saturn	56	thousands
Uranus	27	at least 13
Neptune	13	at least 4

Titania (ty-TAY-nee-uh) is Uranus's largest moon. Its rocks and ice are covered with small craters. There are also many cracks on its surface. Astronomers think Titania was so hot at one time that it was a liquid. The surface may have cooled first. The inside of the moon cooled later. Its shape may have changed, which caused the surface to crack.

Oberon (OH-buh-RAHN) is farther away from Uranus than any of its other major moons. It is a very old moon with many craters. The bottoms of some of the craters seem to be covered in dark material. Astronomers are not sure what this material is. Oberon has a tall mountain that is about 4 miles (6 km) high.

Oberon

Titania

The two moons Oberon and Titania were discovered by William Herschel. He found them in 1787, six years after he discovered Uranus.

Rings and More Rings

Uranus's ring system is not easy to see. Astronomers spotted some rings using telescopes on Earth. The *Voyager 2* spacecraft discovered more rings, bringing the number of known rings up to 11. Then in 2005, the Hubble Space Telescope found two more rings.

Uranus's rings are made up of dust and rocks. Much of this material comes from Uranus's moons. **Meteoroids** continually crash into the planet's moons. When this happens, dust is blasted off the moons' surfaces. This dust spreads out into the rings around the planet. The rings are held in place by the planet's **gravity**.

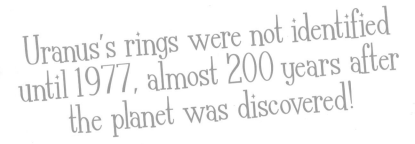

Uranus's rings were not identified until 1977, almost 200 years after the planet was discovered!

This illustration shows the sun shining between Uranus and its rings. The white specks in the background are other stars.

Voyager 2 has been traveling for more than 10,500 days. The purple line shows part of its path through the solar system.

Voyager

Saturn

Jupiter

CHAPTER 6

Mission to Uranus

Voyager 2 is traveling through the solar system at 36,000 miles per hour.

So far, *Voyager 2* has been the only space mission to study Uranus. This space probe was launched on August 20, 1977. A space probe is a spaceship that does not have astronauts on board. Uranus was part of *Voyager 2*'s grand tour of the outer solar system.

Astronomers studied more than 10,000 possible routes for *Voyager 2*.

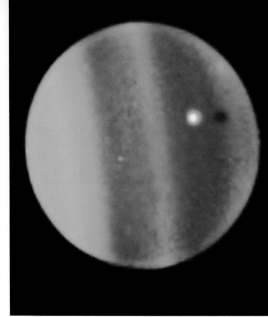

This image was taken by the Hubble Space Telescope on Thursday, August 31, 2006. It shows one of Uranus's moons crossing the face of the planet. The moon cast a shadow on Uranus.

Uranus was not *Voyager 2*'s first stop. The space probe flew by Jupiter, then Saturn to gather information on those planets. Then it went on to Uranus. *Voyager 2* reached Uranus almost 10 years after it was launched. On January 24, 1986, it flew by at a distance of 50,600 miles (81,500 km) from Uranus's cloud tops.

Voyager 2 conducted 10 different experiments. It took about 8,000 pictures of Uranus and its moons and rings. It gathered information on temperature, gases in the atmosphere, gravity, and more. *Voyager 2* discovered 10 new moons that astronomers had not known about.

After leaving Uranus, *Voyager 2* went on to Neptune. Then it started its journey to the outer reaches of our solar system and beyond. In March 2007, *Voyager 2* was nearly 8 billion miles (13 billion km) from Earth. This is more than twice as far from Earth as Uranus is.

Voyager 2 is still sending messages and information to Earth. It is expected to do so until 2020, when its power supply will probably run out.

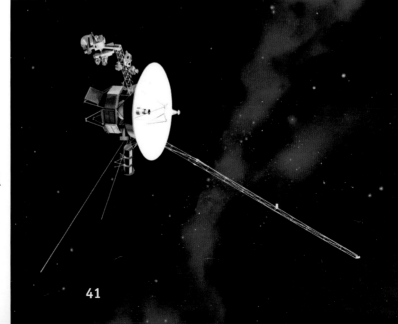

Voyager 2 was the first spacecraft to travel to Uranus and Neptune. An identical spacecraft called Voyager 1 is the most distant human-made object in space.

There is still a lot more to know about Uranus. Scientists would like to know more about Uranus's moons, its weather, and the deep space that surrounds it, for example. Information from new telescopes and other instruments may help scientists answer these questions.

Scientists will continue to observe Uranus through telescopes until a new mission to the planet takes place.

True Statistics

7th planet from the sun

Classification: Gas giant

Discovered: In 1781 by William Herschel

Number of moons: 27

Distance from the sun: About 1.8 billion mi. (2.8 billion km)

Length of a day: About 17 Earth hours

Length of a year: About 84 Earth years

Number of rings: 13

Diameter: 31,764 mi. (51,118 km)

100-pound (45 kg) person on Earth would weigh: 89 lb. (40 kg) on Uranus

Average temperature: −357°F (−216°C)

Gas that makes it look blue: Methane

Did you find the truth?

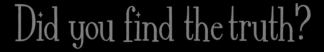 There are no rings around Uranus.

Uranus is the first planet that was discovered by using a telescope.

Resources

Books

Atkinson, Stuart. *Space Travel*. Austin, TX: Raintree Steck-Vaughn, 2002.

Carruthers, Margaret. *The Hubble Space Telescope*. Danbury, CT: Franklin Watts, 2004.

Kerrod, Robin. *Space Probes*. Milwaukee, WI: World Almanac Library, 2005.

Prinja, Raman K. *Comets, Asteroids, and Meteors*. Chicago: Heinemann Library, 2003.

Shearer, Deborah A. *Space Missions*. Mankato, MN: Bridgestone Books, 2003.

Somervill, Barbara A. *The History of Space Travel*. Chanhassen, MN: The Child's World, 2004.

Taylor-Butler, Christine. *Uranus*. Danbury, CT: Children's Press, 2008.

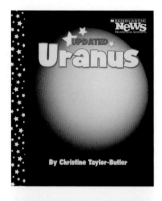

Organizations and Web Sites

Astronomy for Kids—Uranus
www.kidsastronomy.com/uranus.htm
Check out this site for more information about Uranus.

NASA: The Space Place
spaceplace.jpl.nasa.gov
Visit this site for an enjoyable lesson on space.

National Space Society
1620 I Street NW, Suite 615
Washington, DC 20006
202-429-1600
This organization works toward humans living and working
in space.

Places to Visit

Kennedy Space Center
Kennedy Space Center, FL
32899
www.ksc.nasa.gov
Explore NASA's launch
headquarters and learn
more about some of the
organization's space missions.

**Smithsonian National Air
and Space Museum**
Independence Avenue at 4th
Street, SW
Washington, DC 20560
202-633-1000
www.nasm.si.edu
See the world's largest
collection of historic airplanes
and spaceships

Important Words

asteroids (AS-tuh-roidz) – large pieces of rock that orbit the sun

astronomers (uh-STRAW-nuh-murz) – scientists who study the planets, stars, and space

atmosphere (AT-mu-sfihr) – the blanket of gases that surrounds a planet or other object

axis (AK-siss) – an imaginary line that runs through the center of a planet or other object

comets – large chunks of rock and ice that travel around the sun

dwarf planets – bodies in the solar system that orbit the sun, have a constant (nearly round) shape, are not moons, and have orbits that overlap with the orbits of other bodies

fluorescent (flo-RE-snt) – giving off light energy after receiving another form of energy

gravity – a force that pulls two objects together

meteoroids (MEE-tee-uh-roidz) – chunks of rock, metal, or other debris in space that are up to .6 mile (1 km) in size

orbits – travels around an object such as a sun or planet

rotate – to spin on an axis

solar system (SOH-lur SISS-tuhm) – a sun and all the objects that travel around it

Index

About the Author

Award-winning author Elaine Landau has a bachelor's degree from New York University and a master's degree in library and information science from Pratt Institute.

She has written more than 300 non-fiction books for children and young adults. Although Ms. Landau often writes on science topics, she especially likes writing about planets and space.

She lives in Miami, Florida, with her husband and son. The trio can often be spotted at the Miami Museum of Science and Space Transit Planetarium. You can visit Elaine Landau at her Web site: www.elainelandau.com.